Acknowledgements

I thank the Yale University Library, the Folger Shakespeare Library, the Trustees of the British Museum, and the Syndics of the University Library, Cambridge, for permission to publish musical selections from manuscripts in their collections. I also wish to thank Tina Lenert and Jean Wells for invaluable help with the transcriptions and music preparation.

Orpheus playing the vihuela, a plate from Luis Milan's *El Maestro,* (1536).

The Renaissance Guitar.

Selected and transcribed by
Frederick Noad.

International Standard Book Number: 0.8256.9950.9
Library of Congress Catalog Card Number: 73-92400

Book design by Iris Weinstein

Picture research by Jane Dorner
Illustrations on pages 75, 89, and 103 courtesy of Dover Publications.
Photographs on page 73 courtesy of the Warnick County Museum Market Place.
Photographs on page 15 courtesy of the National Galley.
Photographs on page 18 courtesy of B.T. Butsford, Ltd., London.
Photographs on page 18 courtesy of Ashmolean Museum, Oxford.
Music facsimiles and illustrations on pages 4, 12, 16, 17, 29, 40,
44, 56, 60, 71, 83, 106, 115, and 119 courtesy of the British Museum.

Exclusive Distributors:
Music Sales Corporation
225 Park Avenue South, New York, NY 10003 USA
Music Sales Limited
8/9 Frith Street, London W1V 5TZ England
Music Sales Pty. Limited
120 Rothschild Street, Rosebery, Sydney, NSW 2018, Australia

Printed and bound in the United States of America by
Vicks Lithograph and Printing Corporation

Contents

cont'd

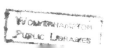

The Renaissance Guitar

Preface

The Frederick Noad Guitar Series is a response to the need of the very large number of players who have mastered basic guitar techniques and want interesting and well written musical selections for further study and enjoyment. There is an enormous amount of music for the guitar, rivaling or surpassing in quantity that for any other instrument. But the quality of both music and fingering varies enormously, and it is probably true that there is more bad or dull music in print for this instrument than for any other.

The reasons for this poor quality are not hard to find. First, few major composers wrote for the guitar since technical difficulties demand that the composer either play the guitar himself or work closely with a player. Second, the many players who wrote music for the guitar were usually poor composers relying on special effects or superficial charm to attract the listener. Third, editors have rarely had the specialized knowledge to recognize a good guitar piece and have printed music for the guitar that would be considered totally inadequate if published for the piano or violin.

It is thus difficult for even the accomplished player to find good music. Outlets for guitar scores are usually confined to major cities; the majority of players must shop from catalogs supplied by publishers and invariably have to discard much of what they buy. Anthologies are few, and in many of these the player responsible for fingering has altered the original score to suit his own taste.

There does exist, however, much fine music, and I think that such music should be presented in reasonably priced and easily accessible editions. This series attempts to meet this goal. The series is conceived in three parts—Renaissance, Baroque and Classical. The books contain original transcriptions as well as recognized favorites and present much music unavailable elsewhere. In addition, I have put each period in perspective and introduced the major composers, forms, and playing styles of the time. The selections are classified in three levels: basic, intermediate, and advanced. Brief notes are given at points of technical difficulty. It is hoped that the learner will find enjoyment in the early sections and that the seasoned player will find material in the more challenging works. However, at all levels I have tried to maintain a high standard of musical interest. The selections have been carefully transcribed from original sources, either manuscript or first edition, and every effort has been made to respect the composer's intention.

These anthologies, however, must inevitably represent the taste of one person. It is impossible to please everyone, but I hope most sincerely that other players will share, at least in part, the pleasure I have found in these selections.

FREDERICK NOAD

Introduction

Although separated in time from us by almost four centuries, the late Renaissance provides a most fruitful and enjoyable source of music for the guitarist. The tunes were lively and straightforward; the forms uncomplicated; and, most important of all, some of the best composers of the period were writing for plucked strings. The later popularity of keyboard instruments relegated the guitar and lute to a relatively minor role in the history of music, but in the Renaissance the repertoire for plucked strings was the largest and most important body of instrumental music.

The music in this collection is drawn from pieces for the vihuela, guitar, lute, bandore, and lyra-viol. To understand both the chronology and character of the repertoire, it is perhaps easiest to discuss it in connection with the instruments for which it was originally written.

Music for the Vihuela

In many ways, the vihuela was the instrument of this period closest to the modern guitar. Its shape was similar, although its body was somewhat smaller and thinner. Its six strings were paired in unison for extra resonance, much like the twelve-string guitar of today, and these pairs are known as "courses."

The vihuela tuning varies from the modern guitar only in the tuning of the third string, which was tuned a semitone lower. Thus by tuning the guitar G string down to F# it is possible to read original music directly.

The actual pitch of the vihuela varied; it ranged from Luis Milan's vague instruction to tune the top string "as high as it will go" to more specific recommendations by the other composers. The range of the top string appears to have been from the E of the modern guitar to an A a fourth higher, though the latter tuning was probably reserved to smaller instruments of shorter string length.

Vihuela

The printed literature exists in eight books which include solo songs and arrangements of choral works, as well as instrumental solos. These works are Luis Milan's *El maestro* (1536); Luis de Narvaez's *Los seys libros del Delphin* (1538); Alonso de Mudarra's *Tres libros de musica en cifra para vihuela* (1546); Enriquez de Valderrábano's *Silva de Sirenas* (1547); Diego Pisador's *Libro de musica de vihuela* (1552); Miguel de Fuenllana's *Orphenica lyra* (1554); Juan Bermudo's *Declaracion de instrumentos* (1555); and Estebán Daza's *El Parnaso* (1576).

Many of the extended pieces which appear in these books are not particularly suitable for modern performance since they tend to amble on in a quite pleasant but not very striking fashion. However, there are some notable exceptions, particularly Mudarra's "Fantasia," in which he imitates the style of a famous harpist of the day, Ludovico. This is reproduced on p.108. Valderrábano is represented by his "Sonnet" on p. 39 which has the charm and feeling of a lullaby. Vocal works include Milan's "Toda mi vida os ame" p.56, for which two accompaniments are given. Against the simple accompaniment the singer would elaborate the vocal line *(hacer garganta)*, but when the guitarist played the ornamental accompaniment the singer would keep to the written notes *(cantar llano)*. "Morenica de me un beso" p.68 by Juan Vasquez, which is found in Fuenllana's *Orphenica lyra,* has great charm and gaiety, and his songs in general stand out as the most interesting of the period.

The vihuela music in these books is printed in tablature rather than conventional musical notation. The six courses of the vihuela are each represented by a line, and a number on the line indicates the fret to be played. The time is indicated above the lines.

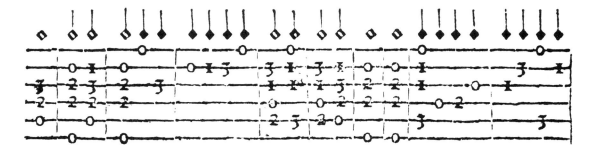

The example shown is the opening of the pavane by Luis Milan transcribed in full on p.40. Note that the time indications give only the period from one note or chord to the next; the player or editor must decide which notes are held over.

The later books used the same form of notation, except that the highest string was represented by the bottom rather than the top line. Milan's arrangement corresponds to French lute tabulature, although the French used letters rather than numbers. The form used by other vihuela composers corresponds to Italian lute tabulature.

The example shown from Narvaez's "Guardame las vacas" illustrates the Italian form. The full transcription of this piece appears on p.78; it is an interesting and melodious example of the earliest form of theme and variations.

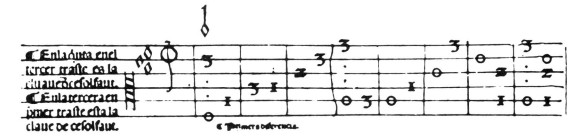

Music for the Guitar

Juan Bermudo, in the work mentioned above, states that the only difference between the vihuela and the guitar was in the number of courses, the guitar having four while the vihuela had six. The tuning of the Renaissance guitar was the same as that of the top four strings of the modern guitar; the actual pitch was usually a tone lower. The strings were usually doubled although the highest string was sometimes a single (as in the lute). The limited amount of strings called for more ingenuity from the composer, and the small surviving literature shows that the challenge was not very well met, at least on the part of the French composers. In addition, the surviving fantasias of the Italian Melchior de Barberiis are disappointing for their poverty of invention.

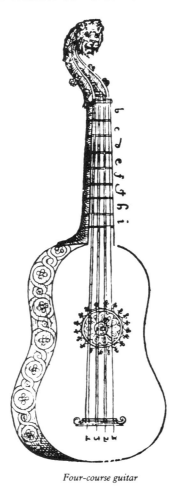

Four-course guitar

A brighter moment from the extensive collections of Adrien Le Roy is given in "Branle de Bourgogne" on p. 30 . But by far the most sophisticated handling of this limited instrument is shown by Miguel de Fuenllana who devotes a section of *Orphenica Lyra* to the guitar. His "Fantasia," transcribed on p. 74 , has the quality of a beautifully executed miniature and leads one to believe that the Spaniards were more familiar than the other nationalities with the guitar. Further evidence for this is afforded by some guitar works in Mudarra's *Tres Libros de Musica* which, although of only average interest, are at least competently constructed.

It is probably correct to assume that the four-course guitar was used mainly for chording in song accompaniment and for this reason was more a popular than a sophisticated instrument.

Music for the Lute

The lute is distinguished from instruments of the guitar family by its pear-shaped body made of a number of curved ribs. The peg head containing the tuning pegs did not project beyond the fingerboard as on a guitar, but was angled back probably for the convenience of the player performing in a confined space with other musicians.

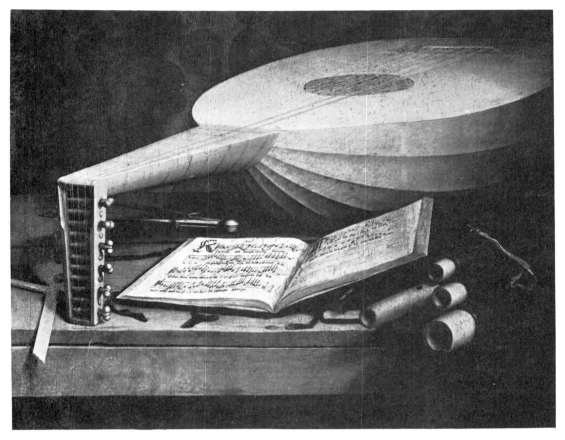

Renaissance lute. Detail from Holbein's *The Ambassadors.*

Its six courses were known by name, the highest being the treble, and the others in descending order the small mean, great mean, contratenor, tenor, and bass.

The music for the lute was written in tablature, the most common forms using letters to indicate the appropriate frets *(a* for open string, *b* for the first fret, and so on).

The tuning of the sixteenth-century lute is comparable to that of the vihuela, the most usual pitch being a third higher than the modern guitar. However, unlike the vihuela, the highest string was not doubled, and later in the century extra courses were added. The seven-course lute had an additional bass pair a fourth below the sixth course (D), and the eight-course had an additional pair one tone below the sixth (F).

The repertoire for the lute is so vast that it is impossible to treat it with any completeness in a work of this sort. It was the uncontested leader of musical instruments of the sixteenth century as many contemporary writings attest. Typical is this extract from a poem commemorating the entry of Queen Anne of Denmark into Edinburgh in 1590—"Sum on Lutys did play and sing / Of instruments the only king."

The collection in this book is largely drawn from the golden age of English lute music (about 1580–1620) although some fine continental composers are represented. It was during this same period that the English "ayre," or lute song, reached its highest point giving us some of the most beautiful songs in the English language.

For the solo pieces the bulk of the sources are in manuscript form and are in fact the handwritten lute books of players of the time. Some, such as the neat and precisely written book of Jane Pickering, are in the same handwriting throughout. In others the handwriting varies; perhaps a visiting lutenist may have been prevailed upon to add a piece to the family book. A particularly interesting example is the Dowland lute book, now in the possession of the Folger Shakespeare Library in Washington, D.C. Beginning with some anonymous but very well constructed beginner's pieces (see "Wilson's Wilde" on p. 26 and "Lesson for Two Lutes" on p.27), later pages contain autograph compositions by John Dowland, the most famous lutenist of the period. The book remained in the Dowland family until this century, when it was sold by M. L. Dowland.

The most complete printed anthology of English lute music was collected by Dowland's son Robert and published in 1610 as *A Variety of Lute Lessons.* The word "lesson" was widely used to mean a solo piece, in the same sense as *etude* or study, and the collection is much more an anthology than an instruction book, although there is some introductory didactic text.

Thomas Robinson's *School of Music* (1610) makes amusing reading; the instruction is in the form of a dialogue between a music master and a knight who has children to be instructed. His book, Robinson claims, will teach anyone to play a piece at first sight ("if it is not too trickified"). The example of his music "Toy for Two Lutes" on p.72 , is pleasant and certainly not "trickified."

Non-English printed sources of solo music include the very large *Thesaurus harmonicus* (1603) of Jean Baptiste Besard, a leading French composer-lutenist, and Georg Fuhrmann's *Testudo Gallo-Germanico* (1615) from which the Mertel piece on p. 50 is derived.

Lute songs often appeared in attractively printed books of the period, in which the pages were so arranged that a group could sit around a table sharing the same book. Most songs have four parts but were equally popular as solo songs to the lute or viola da gamba.

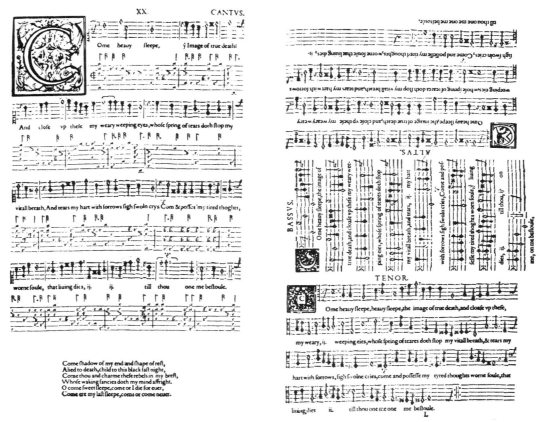

A page from John Dowland's *First Booke of Songes or Ayres,* (1597).

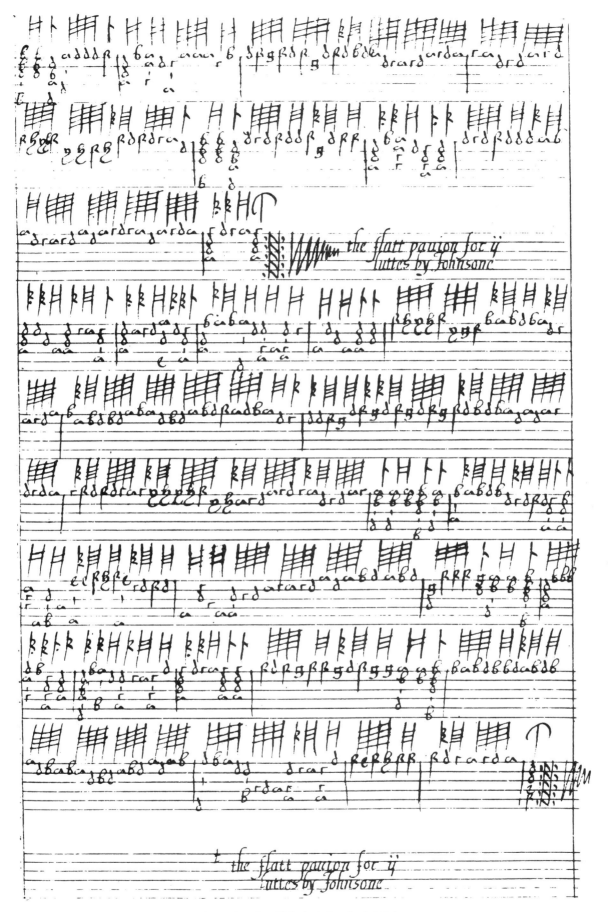

A page from Jane Pickering's *Lute Book*, (1616).

Amid such a treasury of good songs it is hard to select favorites; but I have chosen works that represent a range of feeling, from the heavy melancholy of Dowland's "Come Heavy Sleep" to the lyrical and frivolous "When from My Love" of John Bartlet. I have somewhat reluctantly modernized the Elizabethan spelling of some words where I felt that the meaning of the lyric might otherwise be lost. When sung, the difference in pronunciation is not perceptible.

Music for the Bandore and Lyra-Viol

The bandore (also bandora or pandora) was a metal-strung bass instrument of the cittern family. These instruments were characterized by a flat back and a rounder thinner body than the lute. The music was also written in tablature, and the tuning was comparable to the top five strings of the guitar, the bottom string being one tone lower than the fifth. The example given, "The Night Watch" by Anthony Holborne (p. 61), was chosen more because it was a good popular tune of the time than from a desire to include a work for this instrument, although the bandore was very popular in the instrumental combinations, or "consorts," of the period.

The lyra-viol was a member of the bowed viol family that was used more often for contrapuntal or chorded music rather than the single lines usually associated with these instruments. In fact, any bass viol could be used to play "lyra-way," but the music was customarily played on a slightly smaller instrument which would ease the stretch requirements for the left hand in making chords. After 1600 the increasing virtuosity of viol players appears to have given some challenge to the former supremacy of the lutenists. (See, for example, John Dowland's rather defensive introduction to his *Pilgrim's Solace* in 1612.) "Mr. Southcote's Pavan," the duet for two lyra-viols by Thomas Ford on p. 116, was chosen for the well-balanced and attractive interplay between the two instruments.

Bandore

Lyra-Viol

Form and Style of Performance

The fantasy was the most developed form of purely instrumental piece with no dance association. Many of the contrapuntal devices later used in the fugue are employed, and in general the fantasy represented the most sophisticated writing of the lute composers. Other instrumental pieces of a more lighthearted nature were given fanciful titles such as toy, nothing, jump, and so on.

With the exception of the fantasies the solo forms are predominantly those of dance music. Pavanes and galliards abound, sometimes linked by the same thematic material as in John Johnson's "The Flatt Pavin" (p.93) and his following "Galliard" (p.96). The pavanes were a more stately dance than the galliards, which had leaping steps and a faster pace. It is clear that not all the pieces were intended for dancing; and some, such as Dowland's "Melancholy Galliard" (p.80) would lose their character if performed in strict dance tempo.

The alman (spelled also almain, almayne, and so on) translates literally as "German dance." In this period it was used as the title for pieces in duple time of moderate tempo. In comparing it with the galliard, Thomas Morley wrote, "The Alman is a more heavie daunce than this (fitlie representing the nature of the people [German] whose name it carieth) so that no extraordinary motions are used in the dauncing of it." *(A Plaine and Easie Introduction to* Practicall Musicke, 1597.)

The other principal form is that of theme and variations, usually on a well-known folk melody of the time. Narvaez's "Guardame las vacas" is one of the earliest examples of this form, and English lute music abounds with arrangements of "Walsingham," "Go from My Window," "Greensleeves," "Bonny Sweet Robin," and so on.

There is so much variety of style from piece to piece that individual recommendations have been given in the notes to each composition. However, it is possible to say in general that Renaissance music does not lend itself to a rubato or romantic style of phrasing. This does not mean that a mechanical performance is necessary for authenticity; there is ample opportunity for variation in dynamics, tone, color, and so on. The music is extremely vital, and a dry academic rendering of it is both dull and inappropriate.

Ornamentation has been kept to a minimum, being more a characteristic of the transition to the baroque period. The ornaments are in fact written into the pieces in the form of florid repeats or divisions, and further elaboration succeeds only in gilding the lily.

About the Music

In transcribing these pieces for the guitar, I have tried to produce playable and natural versions for the instrument while keeping every possible part of the original. The lowest courses of the lute have had to be transposed an octave, but since they were little used this is not a serious problem. The music for the four-course guitar and vihuela has necessitated no changes of this kind, and the lyra-viol music lies comfortably on the guitar without alteration.

It has been necessary to transpose the keys of the lute pieces to adapt to the lower pitch of the guitar. Thus the music is not in its true pitch, but it is in its correct relationship to the open strings. Guitarists may wish to remedy this by putting a capodastro on the third fret, which will result in both the correct key and correct relationship to the open strings. Transposing up by any other means makes the music extremely difficult, if not impossible, to play.

The choice of pieces is personal, so there is no particular balance between countries of origin or individual composers. I have invariably preferred to choose music for qualities that appeal to me rather than suffer the restriction of even representation.

I have not presumed to correct these excellent composers in any way except in the case of obvious typographical errors. However, I have occasionally dropped a note in a chord where the chord was easy and natural to the lute but difficult and strained on the guitar. This is from a desire to preserve the continuity of a phrase or cadence, which I feel serves the composer's intention better than some technical contortion to save a note. The problem can often be solved by tuning the third string down a semitone, but inexperienced players have such a resistance to doing this that I have in general avoided the expedient. However, two pieces for the advanced player, the fantasias by Dowland and Mudarra, are fingered this way to ease technical problems. In all cases, the suggested fingering is editorial.

Although scholarship has its important place, I feel that the main purpose of publishing music is to enable it to be played and listened to with enjoyment. Hence the study notes are directed to the player to assist him in learning the piece, and biographical and musicological references are brief. The player interested in further reading will find material suggested in the notes.

Renaissance duet

Spagnoletta

This piece, taken from an Italian manuscript source by the nineteenth-century musi-cologist Oscar Chilesotti, is an example of the popular tune *Españoleta*, or "Little Spanish Tune." An orchestrated version of the tune may be heard in Joachin Rodrigo's *Fantasia para un gentilhombre* for guitar and orchestra.

The tempo should be moderate, about ♩ = 116, but with a lilt and no heaviness.

[1] *A slight stress on the first beat here will help to establish the changed pattern of phrase.*

Anonymous

Tanz

This lighthearted dance is taken from *Testudo Gallo-Germanico*. The word *Testudo* means lute, or more literally "tortoise shell," from the myth that the first lute was the result of a tortoise decaying. Its entrails were stretched across the shell, and when plucked they had a musical sound. This unlikely story is widely quoted in early treatises.

As the bass pattern is the same throughout, it may be practiced by itself before adding the melody. All three bass notes should be played with the thumb, the melody with alternating free strokes.

Suggested tempo is a brisk $\quartnote = 176$.

6th to D

Georg Fuhrmann

Branle Gay

Besard was a highly respected French lutenist who was also trained as a lawyer. His large collection of his own and other composers' music was published in Cologne in 1603.

The branle was a lively country dance, often characterized by an unchanging or "drone" bass. Like the preceding piece, this dance depends for its effectiveness on a fast tempo, preferably about ♩ = 144.

1. *The third finger is important here to release the second finger for the E bass.*
2. *Notice the small minus sign by the first finger indication. This means that the first finger travels from the G♯ to the A without losing contact with the string. It does not mean that the slide should be audible.*

6th to D

Jean Baptiste Besard

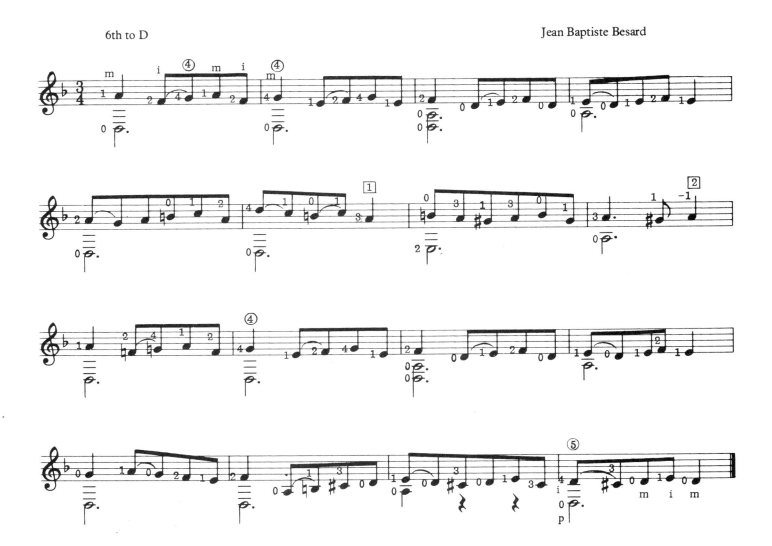

24

Toy

This piece is from the very large manuscript collection known as D.D.2.11 in the Cambridge University Library, dating probably from the last decade of the Sixteenth-century. Little is known about Francis Cutting except the popularity and high caliber of his music.

In musical terms a toy was, logically enough, something to play with and enjoy, in much the same sense that "recreation" was a title given to later pieces.

Suggested tempo is ♩ = 144.

1. *Remember to take a full bar here (rather than only five strings) in preparation for the following chord.*
2. *An accent here will bring out the interesting cross-rhythm.*

Francis Cutting

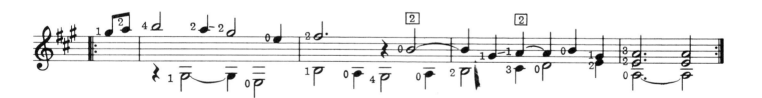

Wilson's Wilde

This piece is from the Dowland lute book. Although easy to play, it is a very effective composition because of the amount of variety in a simple framework. Each of three themes is followed by an ornamented repeat; if the themes are treated with a sustained quality, the repeats may be given an interesting contrast by being played with a brisk attack.
Suggested tempo is ♩ = 152.

Anonymous

Lesson For Two Lutes

Taken from the same manuscript as the preceding piece, this delightful but simple duet should present no technical difficulties if the fingering is strictly followed. A comfortable andante tempo is suggested, about ♩ = 88.

Anonymous

Shall I Come Sweet Love To Thee

Although Campion was not a professional musician, having trained first in law and later in medicine, his poetry and music are among the finest examples of the period. This song is taken from his first *Book of Ayres*. He published four books of "ayres" altogether and shared another with Philip Rosseter. In an introduction he wrote, "These Ayres were for the most part framed at first for one voice with the lute or viol, but upon occasion they have since been filled with more parts, which who so please may use, who like not may leave."

The song should be taken at a gentle tempo to fit the lyric. The singer may wish to ornament one of the verses; a typical example of florid ornamentation is given for this song in the *New Oxford History of Music* (vol. 4, edited by Gerald E. Abraham, 1968, p. 217).

6th to D

Thomas Campion

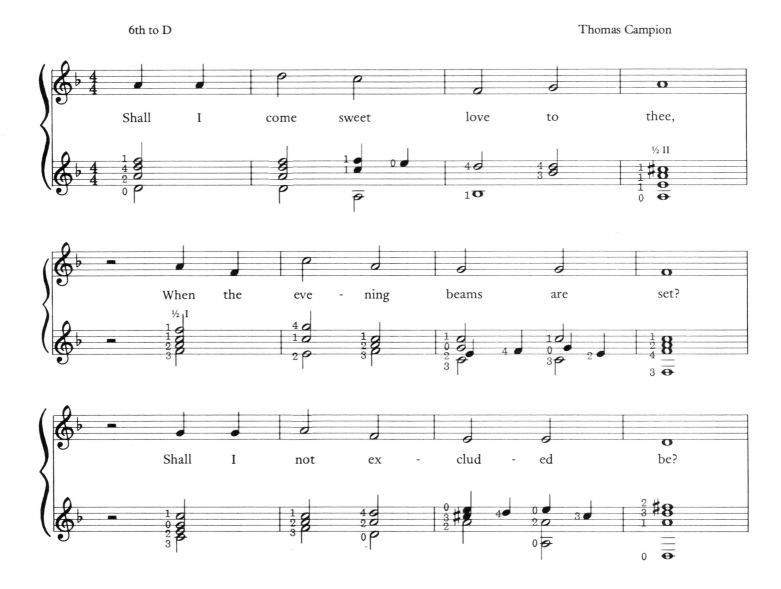

Will you find no fain - ed let?

Let me not for pit - y more, Tell the

long, long hours, Tell the long hours at your door.

Who can tell what thief or foe,
In the cover of the night,
For his prey will work my woe;
Or through wicked soul despite,
So may I die unredressed,
Ere my long, long love,
Ere my long love be possessed.

But to let such dangers pass,
Which a lover's thoughts disdain,
'Tis enough in such a place,
To attend love's joys in vain.
Do not mock me in thy bed,
While these cold, cold nights,
While these cold nights freeze me dead.

Branle De Bourgogne

Taken from Le Roy's *First Book of Tablature for the Guitar* (1551), this country dance is one of the earliest examples of printed guitar music.

An extra stress should be given to the first beat of each measure to give a dance feeling, particularly to the single A beginning measure five, and wherever this figure is repeated.

Suggested tempo is a lively ♩ = 120.

Adrien Le Roy

The Parlement

From the Dowland manuscript, this piece seems to be based on *Kemp's Jig,* a popular tune of the time associated with Will Kemp, the famous English comic actor and dancer.

Suggested tempo is brisk, about ♩ = 144.

1. *It is important to release the third finger from the low C at this point to avoid an ugly clash with the upper C♯. The change of key is somewhat sudden, but it is helped by stressing the C♯.*

6th to D

Anonymous

If My Complaints Could Passions Move

This song is from Dowland's *First Book of Songs or Ayres*, originally published in 1597. By the standards of the time it was a most successful book; and several of the songs, including this one, were highly popular in solo lute and instrumental versions. The instrumental title for this piece was "Master Piper's Galliard."

The tempo should be comfortable but not too slow.

John Dowland

O Love, I live and ___ die in thee;

Thy grief in my deep sighs still

speaks; Thy wounds do fresh - ly ___

bleed in me; My heart for

thy un - kind - ness breaks,

Can love be rich and yet I want?
Is love my judge and yet am I condemned?
Thou plenty hast, yet me dost scant;
Thou made a god, and yet thy power condemned?
That I do live it is thy power,
That I desire it is thy worth,

If love doth make men's lives too sour,
Let me not love, nor live henceforth.
Die shall my hopes but not my faith
That you, that of my fall shall hearers be,
May here despair, which truly saith:
I was more true to Love than Love to me.

Volt

This very popular piece was untitled in the Dowland manuscript but appears elsewhere under the title of *Volt* or *La volta*. It appears frequently in Italian lute sources and was probably originally Italian.

Suggested tempo is ♩ = 116.

1 *The only technical problem lies in the first two measures, where the change from the second to fifth position should be made evenly and without hurry.*

6th to D   Anonymous

Recercate Concertante

To make this attractive duet, Matelart took a lute fantasia of the famous Italian composer Francesco da Milano and added a second part to it. He published his duet version in 1559. The upper part may be played as a solo. Players interested in exploring more of this music are referred to Arthur Ness's very scholarly and complete work *The Lute Music of Francesco da Milano* (Harvard University Press, 1970), which gives tablature and keyboard transcription.

Suggested tempo is ♩ = 80.

Francesco da Milano & Joanne Matelart

Sonnet

This piece was published in 1547 in Valderrábano's *Silva de Sirenas*. Little is known about the composer, despite exhaustive research by Emilio Pujol, who has worked extensively transcribing and editing all vihuela composers.

Suggested tempo is ♩ = 84.

1. *In order to sustain the E the first finger should be pushed down to cover the A without leaving the fourth string.*

Enriquez de Valderrábano

Pavan

This pavan is from *El Maestro* (1535). Luis Milan was a courtier in the viceregal court of Germaine de Foix at Valencia, a scene of social and cultural elegance. He was also the author of *El cortesano,* patterned on the *Libro del Cortegiano,* Castiglione's famous book of court manners. Milan portrays himself somewhat favorably as a highly talented nobleman.

His instructions state that the pavan should be played with the measure somewhat fast. He also indicates that the complete piece may be repeated once or twice, but this suggestion need not be taken literally. I would suggest a rather grandiose approach with a tempo about ♩ = 152.

1 *It is a little awkward to sustain the A, but it is worth the effort.*

2 *Be sure to play the high A loudly enough for it to sustain. A crescendo up to this point is effective.*

3 *This passage should be practiced separately so that tempo is not lost here.*

Pavan

Luis Milan

Fantasia

This piece (originally untitled) was transcribed by Oscar Chilesotti from a Sixteenth-century manuscript lute book. It is chosen here as a straightforward example of a common style of piece which was purely instrumental and unrelated to dance forms. The aim of the player is to bring out the contrapuntal (multiline) quality of the piece by carefully sustaining tied and held notes for their full value. It is important to recognize the original tune as it reoccurs in other voices. The "Fantasia" seems to sound well at a stately ♩ = 76.

Anonymous

The Round Battle Galliard

Dowland was perhaps the most famous lutenist of his day, and his works were extensively published abroad as well as in England. For a marvelously thorough work on this composer, the reader is referred to Diana Poulton, *John Dowland* (Faber Music Ltd., London, 1972).

This piece is great fun to play. Much of Dowland is steeped in Elizabethan melancholy, but this lively dance seems full of humor. It comes from the Dowland lute book.

Suggested tempo is ♩ = 104.

1 *This is an awkward stretch, but it is possible to hold the chord.*

2 *The fingering seems unnatural, but this is one of the cases where in lute tuning there was no problem. On the whole it does not seem worth the inconvenience of tuning down the third string to facilitate this measure, but for those who wish to try it, a third string tuned to F♯ instead of G will take out much of the difficulty of this passage and the following cadence.*

John Dowland

Never Weather Beaten Sail

This song is from Campion's second *Book of Ayres*. Campion is mentioned above in the study notes on p. 28. The chord changes are a little more difficult than the preceding song, and careful attention should be given to the fingering. A moderate tempo seems appropriate, but it should not be allowed to drag.

Thomas Campion

Nev - er weath - er beat - en sail more will - ing bent to shore,

Nev - er tir - ed pil - grims' limbs af - fect - ed slum - ber more;

Than my wearied spright now longs To fly out of my trou-bled breast. Oh come quick-ly, oh come quick-ly, Oh come quick-ly sweet-est Lord, And take my soul to rest.

Ever blooming are the joys of heaven's high paradise,
Cold age deafs not there our ears,
Nor vapor dims our eyes;
Glory there the sun outshines,
Whose beams the blessed only see;
Oh come quickly, oh come quickly,
Oh come quickly Glorious Lord,
And raise my spright to thee.

La Rossignol

The title of this song translates as "The Nightingale," and imitations of bird calls and a well-balanced dialogue between the instruments make this one of the most interesting duets from Jane Pickering's lute book. It is in fact one of my favorites from any period, being simple to play and full of charm.

Suggested tempo is ♩ = 96.

1. *This fingering may seem curious, but it much facilitates the move to the second position bar as the third finger may be left on the B.*
2. *The ornament here is effective as a chirrup in the bird call.*
3. *Lift the bar to allow the open string to sound without taking off the first and third fingers.*

Anonymous

47

Tarleton's Resurrection

This is Dowland in his more melancholy vein. The piece is in fact a lament for the famous clown Richard Tarleton, believed by some to be the person Shakespeare had in mind when he wrote the "Alas, poor Yorick!" speech in *Hamlet*. The source is a manuscript lute book known as the *Wickambrook* now in the possession of Yale University.

The melody is very beautiful, and should be given a singing quality. The piece is in fact easier to play than it looks on paper.

Suggested tempo is ♪ = 76.

John Dowland

Intermediate Music

Ballet

Like "Tanz", this piece is from Fuhrmann's *Testudo Gallo-Germanico*. It is in complete contrast to the English lute music, but it has a well-constructed charm of its own. Probably a fairly brisk tempo is appropriate, particularly to avoid tediousness in the last six measures. I would suggest ♩ = 88.

1 *It is important to notice the move back to the first position here.*
2 *This is a difficult change, but the fourth finger helps to guide the hand.*
3 *Be sure to lay the full bar down for the C♯ .*

6th to D

Elias Mertel

Galliard

This piece is from the Cambridge University manuscript lute book D.D. 5.78. Players interested in discovering more of Holborne's music should see *The Complete Works of Anthony Holborne,* edited by Maszkata Kanazana (Harvard University Press, 1967). This work contains tablature and piano transcription.

Although many galliards reflect their dance origin and sound well with a brisk strict rhythm, this piece is one of those that seem more lyrical and therefore effective if played with a sustained melodic quality. The suggested tempo is ♩ = 66.

1 *The second finger on the low F♯ is a stretch, but seems preferable to jumping the third finger over the B.*

6th to D

Anthony Holborne

51

The Cobbler

This colorful piece is from the Dowland lute book, and introduces a popular form of variation on a folk tune. The tune was printed in John Playford's *The Dancing Master* (7th ed.—1686), showing that it was still popular over half a century later than this manuscript version. Words for the song are given in William Chappell's *Popular Music of the Olden Time* (Vol. 1, 1855, p. 278).

The varied rhythms imply the background tap of the shoemaker's hammer. Cobblers were traditionally merry, and the suggested tempo is ♩ = 126.

1. *This cross-fingering is necessary to make a smooth transition to the next chord. The melody should be emphasized over the accompaniment.*
2. *A stress on the first and third beats of this passage helps to emphasize the rhythm.*

The Cobbler

Anonymous

Alman

This is a lively contrast to the preceding piece. The word *Alman* is the same as *Allemande*, or German (dance).

The manuscripts contain much solo music of both Robert Johnson (who also wrote many songs) and of his father, John. Robert's music is characteristically simpler and more melodic than the sophisticated compositions of his father.

Suggested tempo is ♩ = 108.

1 *It is important to place the full bar down for the F♯ , which takes the difficulty out of the fast change.*

Robert Johnson

Galliard

Rosseter is probably best known for his songs, which he published in conjunction with his friend and fellow composer Thomas Campion. However, a number of his compositions for solo lute survive in manuscript form.

This was almost certainly misnamed a galliard in Jane Pickering's book. It does not seem to fit in three time as indicated in the tablature, and I have rebarred it in four. Suggested tempo is a relaxed ♩ = 69.

1 *This chord seems a wide spread, but it is quite frequently used in lute music.*

2 *This is a hard stretch, but it can be done and the effect is better with the low G sustained.*

Philip Rosseter

Toda Mi Vida Os Amé

Like "Pavan" on p. 41, this song is from Luis Milan's *El Maestro*.

Two accompaniments were given, the instruction being that with the simple accompaniment the singer could ornament the song. However, when the guitarist played the more elaborate accompaniment, the singer was instructed to sing the song plainly.

A translation of the words—not intended for singing—is:

> All my life I have loved you.
> If you love me, I know it not.
> I well know that you hold love
> In disaffection and forgetfulness.
> I know that I am shunned
> Since feeling your disfavor,
> And forever I will love you.
> If you love me, I know it not.

Luis Milan

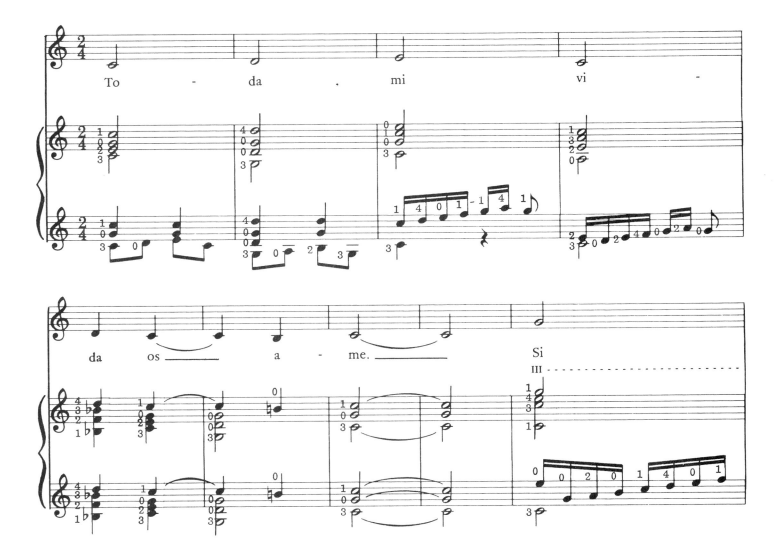

56

me a - ma - ys   yo _____

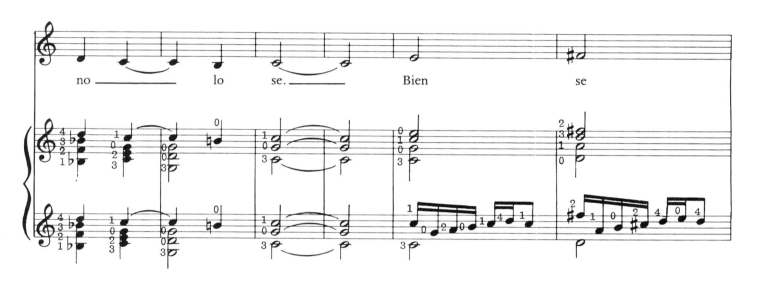

no _____ lo se. ___ Bien   se

que   te - neys __ a - mor _____

Al des - a - mor y al

ol - vi - do. ___ Se que soy

a - bor - re - ci - do ___ Ya

que   sa - be   el   dis - fa -

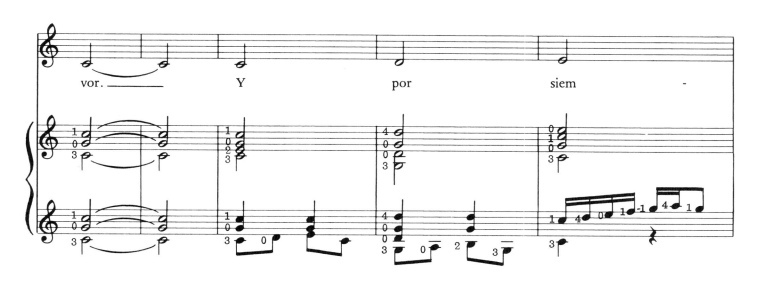

vor. _____ Y   por   siem -

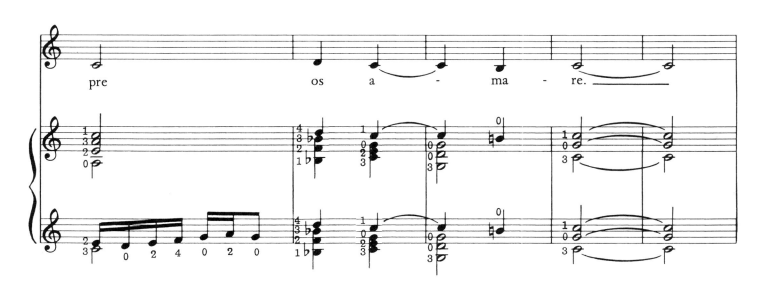

pre   os   a - ma - re. _____

The Night Watch

Holborne wrote versions for both lute and bandore of this piece, which has the air of a popular tune. It makes a pleasant contrast with Holborne's "Galliard," if they are performed as a pair.

The harmonic structure is quite full, which entails some practice to negotiate the chord changes smoothly, but it should be possible to achieve a tempo of about ♩ = 104.

Anthony Holborne

Drewrie's Accordes

This duet is taken from Jane Pickering's lute book, and another version exists in the earlier book of William Ballet under the title *Toy for the Lutes*.

There is a well-balanced interplay between the instruments and considerable scope for a variety of dynamics. Where a theme is stated by one instrument and then exactly imitated by the other, it is often effective to make the statement strong and the imitation a softer echo.

Suggested tempo is ♩ = 138.

[1] *From here to the end there is a series of imitations of bell sounds, probably those of the chimes of London churches. A ringing sound and echoing imitation are particularly pleasing here.*

Anonymous

Air

From the same source as "Toy" by Francis Cutting, this untitled air of Dowland has great charm. It is a little harder to play on the guitar than on the lute, and some players may wish to try it with the third string down to F♯.

Suggested tempo is ♩ = 72.

1. *Here is the principal trouble spot. The first finger has to move as smoothly as possible from the C♯ to the low B. The secret is to do it deliberately without trying to rush it.*
2. *This is a curious voicing of this chord, but it is a very common one in lute music and therefore is a characteristic sound.*
3. *Here is another practice spot; remember to keep the first finger on the previous F♯.*

John Dowland

Go From My Window

This song is from the Dowland manuscript. Like "The Cobbler," it was a popular folk song. In Francis Beaumont's *Knight of the Burning Pestle,* old Merrythought sings:

> Go from my window, love, go;
> Go from my window, my dear;
> The wind and the rain
> Will drive you back again,
> You cannot be lodged here.

Chappell's book, mentioned in the note on p. 52, gives further information about this song on p. 140.

Technically the piece should not present too much difficulty provided that care is taken to notice where the fingering indicates a change from first to second position or the reverse.

There is considerable variety in the variations, and the rhythmic differences should be emphasized for contrast. Suggested tempo is ♩ = 96.

Anonymous

Morenica Da Me Un Beso

This song is a lighthearted dialogue between lovers; the translation is—
  "Dark-haired girl, give me a kiss."
  "What's this about?"
  "What you just heard."
  "Away with you! Don't be so bold,
  I'm not just anyone you know."
  "Give me what I ask for, don't be so unkind.
  You make my life a torment
  And since I am your prisoner
  Give me a kiss!"
  "And I ask you a favor,
  Away with you!"

The version for voice and vihuela is from Fuenllana's *Orphenica lyra*. Technically the accompaniment should give no problem except that it should be played quite fast.

A delightful recording of this song has been made by Victoria de los Angeles (Angel 35888) in the collection *Spanish Songs of the Renaissance.*

Juan Vasquez

ques - to que has o - i - do, oxe a - fue - ra!

No se - ais tan a - tre - vi - do,

Mi - ra que no soy quien

quie - ra, Que no____ soy quien quie - ra,

Da - me lo que te de - man - do, No

de mer - ced te lo pi - do, Oxe a - fue - ra!

No se - ais tan a - tre - vi - do,

Mi - ra que no soy quien

quie - ra, Que no _____ soy quien quie - ra!

Iuan vazquez a tres! Orphenica Lyra. Libro.V. Fo. cxxxiij

Villanci-
co a tres.

Orenica dame vn

71

Toy For Two Lutes

This technically straightforward duet from Robinson's *The Schoole of Musicke* (1603) provides a pleasant recreation. The players should reverse parts at the repeat points.
Notice that most of the sixteenth-note runs will come out best if started with the M finger.
Suggested tempo is ♩ = 84.
|1| *It is not possible to sustain the bass D for more than two counts with this fingering, however the dotted half note shows the intention of the lute original.*

Thomas Robinson

Lute by Hans Frei, dated 1550.

Fantasia

An interesting example of music for the four-string guitar, this piece was published in 1554 in Fuenllana's *Orphenica lyra*. Although blind, the composer was one of the most celebrated players of his time and held a position as musician to the Marquesa de Tarifa. The "Fantasia" shows a more imaginative use of the limited four strings than other published works for guitar during this period. The principal challenge lies in sustaining each voice for its true value.

Suggested tempo is ♩ = 132.

[1] *At this point the first finger should bar the C and the first string F so that the C can be sustained.*

Miguel de Fuenllana

Greensleeves

Greensleeves, one of the most popular tunes in history, was already a favorite in Elizabethan times. It was twice mentioned in Shakespeare's *Merry Wives of Windsor,* and first appeared in the stationer's register of 1580 when Richard Jones had licensed to him "A new Northern Dittye of the Lady Greene Sleeves." There is, however, evidence that the tune is of much earlier origin, perhaps in Henry VIII's time, this registration and the many that followed it being evidence of a new wave of popularity in the late sixteenth-century.

In the following century it was adopted during the revolution by the cavaliers, who wrote many political songs to this tune, and in 1728 appeared again as one of the melodies selected for the *Beggar's Opera.*

One of the earliest instrumental settings occurs in William Ballet's manuscript lute book (late sixteenth-century), and a transcription of this is included in Brian Jeffery's *Elizabethan Popular Music,* (Oxford University Press, 1966). The same author has transcribed a duet version from the Dowland lute book in his Elizabethan Duets (Schott and Co. Ltd., 1970).

Cutting's version lies very well on the guitar and is a pleasure to play. The manuscript of this is now in the British Museum (Add. 31392).

Suggested tempo is a lilting ♪ = 138.

1 *This is a common chord on the lute which makes some demand on the left hand, but it is possible with practice.*

2 *Note the fourth finger, which makes a necessary change of position for the quick move to the D chord.*

3 *The first finger is necessary if the B is to sustain. It is an awkward jump from the previous chord, which may be played staccato to allow for this.*

Francis Cutting

Guardame Las Vacas

This composition is interesting as one of the first printed examples of theme and variations. It is taken from Narvaez's *Los seys libros del Delphin.* Like many early Spanish folk themes, its importance lies as much in its chord sequence as in its melody, and the thread of continuity from variation to variation exists mainly in the repeated harmonic structure. Suggested tempo is ♩ = 144.

1. *A staccato approach is suggested in the upper part for a marked contrast.*
2. *For purposes of speed, players may wish to play only the F♯, allowing the left-hand slide to sound the G♯ .*
3. *A half bar should be placed for the G♯ covering four strings in preparation for the following run.*

Luis de Narvaez

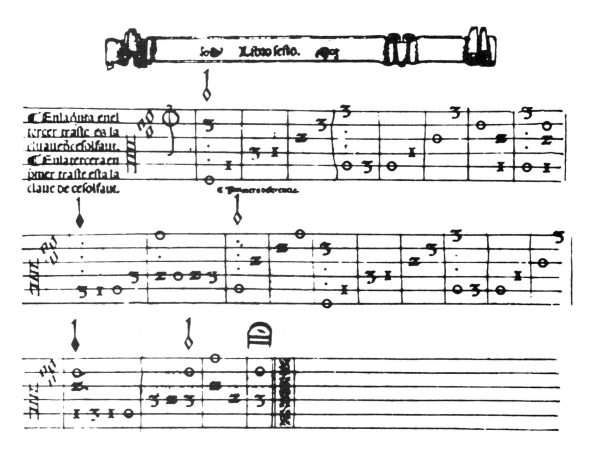

Melancholy Galliard

The prime source for this piece is the Cambridge lute book D.D. 2 11. One of Dowland's most intense compositions, it is a galliard in name only, as it seems quite unsuitable for dance treatment; in fact, a slow brooding approach is indicated. Suggested tempo is ♩ = 58.

1. *This passage, which reoccurs several times, could be taken with a series of half bars with the F chord in the third position. However, I feel that remaining in the fifth position gives a smoother transition to the C chord which begins the following measure.*

2. *Although the D (high D) is intended to be sustained, there seems to be no way to do this without contortion.*

John Dowland

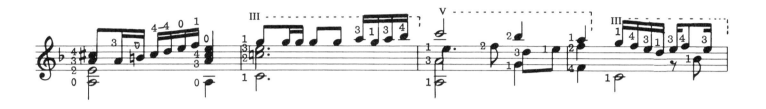

When To Her Lute Corinna Sings

This song of Campion's is from Rosseter's *Book of Ayres,* published in 1601. It has great charm when performed with a light touch, and the last four measures have a most interesting interplay between voice and instrument.

1️⃣ *The third position is necessary in preparation for the following chord, but it may be easier to place both third and fourth fingers at this point.*

2️⃣ *The original was an octave lower; unfortunately, this is impossible on the guitar. The stretch is worth it to sustain the chord.*

Thomas Campion

When to her lute Co - rin - na sings, Her voice re - vives ___ the lead - en strings,

And doth in high - est notes ap - pear, As an - y chal - lenged e - cho clear;

But when she doth of mourn - ing speak, Ev'n with her sighs, her sighs,

her sighs the strings do break, The ___ strings do break.

And as her lute doth live or die,
Led by her passion, so must I,
For when of pleasure she doth sing,
My thoughts enjoy a sudden spring;
But if she doth of sorrow speak,
Ev'n from my heart, my heart, my heart the strings do break,
The strings do break.

Hen to her lute Corrina sings, her voice reuiues the lea- den stringes,

and doth in highest noates appeare as any challeng'd eccho cleere, but when she doth of mour-

ning speake, eu'n with her sighes her sighes, ii. the strings do breake the strings do breake.

And as her lute doth liue or die,
Led by her passion, so must I,
For when of pleasure she doth sing,
My thoughts enioy a sodaine spring,
But if she doth of sorrow speake,
Eu'n from my hart the strings doe breake.

Galliard

From Mudarra's *Tres libros de musica en cifra para vihuela* (1546), this galliard has a strong dance feeling and should be played in strict tempo. Actual speed will be governed by the sixteenth-note runs.

Suggested tempo is ♩ = 84.

1 *The original has an additional G an octave lower.*

2 *This measure and the next contain the major technical difficulties of the piece. The fingering seems somewhat strange, but this seems to be the best solution.*

Alonso de Mudarra

Mrs. Anne Harecourt's Galliard

Like Dowland, Pilkington took his bachelor's degree in music at Oxford. He later became rector of St. Bridget's Church in Chester. His *First Book of Songs* was published in 1605, and one of these songs (p. 106) is included later in this book. This galliard is from the Cambridge lute book (D.D. 2.11).

The structure of this galliard makes it unlikely that it was played fast, and indeed it seems to have a wistful charm at a moderate tempo, about ♩ = 80.

1. *At both these points I have simplified the lute original to ease the flow of the piece.*
2. *Note the change to the fourth finger to free the third for the following chord.*

Francis Pilkington

Advanced Music

The King Of Denmark's Galliard

This short version of Dowland's galliard for his onetime patron Christian IV of Denmark is taken from the book *Lachrimae or Seven Tears.* The compositions in it were for viols and lute, the lute parts being somewhat simpler than the extended solo arrangements.

I suggest a vigorous, imperial approach at a tempo of about ♩ = 108.

1. *The right-hand thumb plays both the low A and E.*
2. *The change to the fourth finger is an important preparation for the chord that begins the next measure.*

John Dowland

Queen Elizabeth's Galliard

A fitting companion to the previous piece is Dowland's tribute to his own queen. This piece appears in the *Variety of Lute Lessons,* published by Dowland's son, Robert. Of majestic structure, it evokes fanfares and trumpet calls, and the change to 9/8 time is particularly effective.

Suggested tempo is ♩ = 88.

1. *This is an unusual arrangement for the right hand, but it is not particularly difficult when it is clear in the mind.*
2. *The ligados here and elsewhere in the piece are editorial and may be omitted. However, in this passage they seem to emphasize the relationship to the first theme.*
3. *A staccato approach to the melody followed by a stress on the high B helps to establish the new rhythm. Three eighth notes now take the same time as a quarter note in the previous section.*
4. *A stress at these points helps to emphasize the cross-rhythm.*

John Dowland

Lady Hammond's Alman

In Elizabethan times it was customary to show appreciation to patrons by dedicating a composition to them, and this piece and the one which follows are an example of charming "gifts" of this sort. The source is the Cambridge Manuscript D.D.2.11.

1 *The slightly unusual fingering of this measure is quite easy with practise and facilitates the execution of the chord on the second beat.*

Suggested tempo is ♩ = 66.

John Dowland

Lady Hunsdon's Alman

This version is taken from the Dowland lute book, and it appears to be in his own handwriting, floridly signed "Bachelor of Musick." Suggested tempo is a lively ♩ = 66. Some passages are crossed out in favor of quite different alternatives. Since some of the variants appear to be improvements on the original, they are given here.

For this measure the crossed out Dowland version is

The lute book D.D.5.78 gives

2 *This is a difficult passage on the guitar, but it is possible if the fourth finger is anchored to the third string for the first three beats of the measure.*

3 *The alternative in D.D.5.78 is*

which has a nice spring to it.

4 *In the original the F♯ was an octave lower.*

5 *This measure is replaced by two in D.D.5.78 as follows—*

Lady Hunsdon's Alman

6th to D

John Dowland

The Flatt Pavin

John Johnson was lutenist to the Royal Chapel from 1581 to his death in 1595. His
Flatt Pavin was an extremely popular piece and reoccurs in manuscript lute books.
This duet version is from Jane Pickering's book.
Suggested tempo is ♩ = 88.
The technique is straightforward providing that care is taken to observe fingerings
which involve a change of position.

1 *Use the end of the first finger, as if about to bar, then place the tip on the B and lift the*
   other end to sound the open string.

John Johnson

Galliard To The Flatt Pavin

This piece first appeared in Jane Pickering's lute book. Containing the same thematic material as the "Flatt Pavin," this galliard may be programmed effectively with it. This type of pairing was more common on the Continent than in England, but there are nevertheless many examples in the English lute school.
Suggested tempo is ♩ = 96.

John Johnson

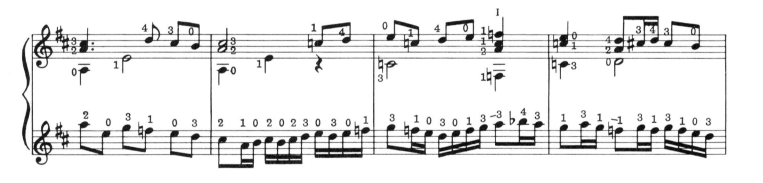

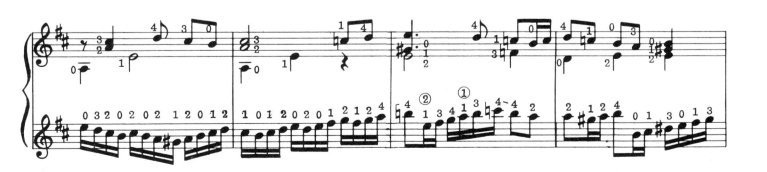

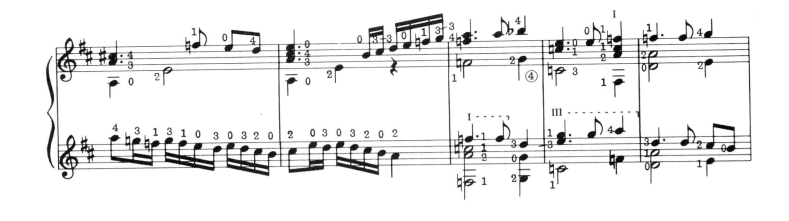

As I Went To Walsingham

Walsingham was a popular folk song arranged by almost all the Elizabethan composers. The song, from the Cambridge lute book (D.D.2.11), relates to the traditional pilgrimage to the Church of Our Lady at Walsingham, Norfolk, which was a shrine famous for miracles. Since the priory there was dissolved in 1538, the tune is clearly a very old one.

In *Popular Music of the Olden Time* William Chappell gives the following words—

>   As I went to Walsingham,
>   To the shrine with speed,
>   Met I with a jolly palmer
>   In a pilgrim's weed.

A palmer was a monk who went from shrine to shrine.

Suggested tempo is ♩ = 80.

Although some of the chord changes need practice, the leisurely tempo should make this piece not too difficult technically.

1 *The high B can be held over on the lute, but it is unfortunately not possible to do so on the guitar. A crescendo up to this point is effective.*

Anonymous

Come Heavy Sleep

This is one of the most beautiful songs in Dowland's first book. Full of brooding melancholy, it represents this composer in his most intense mood. The first words of the second verse have been rearranged to the order suggested by Dr. E. W. Fellowes. A slow sustained tempo is necessary.

Benjamin Britten's beautiful Nocturnal, opus 70, for solo guitar is based on this theme, which appears in the final movement.

1. *The fingering may seem strange, but it is necessary to sustain the chord. Note that the third finger is already in position from the previous chord.*

2. *This is a similar situation to the one just noted; the second finger is already in position from the preceding chord.*

John Dowland

Come shape of rest,
And shadow of my end,
Allied to Death, child to this black-faced, black-faced night;
Come thou and charm these rebels in my breast,
Whose waking fancies doth my mind affright.

O come sweet sleep, or I die forever;
Come ere my last sleep comes,
Come ere my last sleep comes,
Or come, or come thou never.

Almain

The catchy tune and repeated versions of this allemande indicate that it was one of Cutting's more popular pieces. This version is based on the British Museum manuscript Add. 31392.

Suggested tempo is a lively ♩ = 132.

1. *After the initial A the first finger forms a three-string half bar without lifting off.*
2. *There is a temptation to use the first finger, but I think the G♯ sounds better held for the extra half beat. The E in the original was an octave higher.*
3. *The original had an F♯ above the D♯; this is possible but awkward.*
4. *Lift the end of the bar to sound the A while holding the F♯.*

Francis Cutting

Mrs. Taylor's Galliard

This is such a good piece that I am surprised not to have seen it in print before. In the manuscript—Cambridge D.D. 5 78—the first two measures appeared to be all quarter notes. However, the piece seemed to have the structure of a dance galliard, which, because of a leap at the fourth step from the beginning, often has a dotted note on the fourth beat. A reexamination of the original revealed what looked like random ink spots over certain notes; on treating these as dotted notes however, a consistent and convincing pattern emerged.

Suggested tempo is ♩ = 88.

1. *Lift just part of the bar to sound the open A.*
2. *This is a typical lute fingering, but guitarists may prefer a second position bar.*
3. *Use the end of the first finger as if about to bar. This is an unusual but very useful technique when the bar is to follow.*

Philip Rosseter

Rest Sweet Nymphs

This charming lullaby is from Pilkington's *First Book of Songs,* published in 1605. The change of tempo is as printed in the original, but the stress falls on the second beat of the measure in the 3/4 section. I suggest a light andantino tempo.

Francis Pilkington

thies, Lul - la lul - la - by, Lul - la lul - la - by,

Sleep sweet - ly, sleep sweet - ly, Let noth - ing af - fright ye,

In calm con - tent - ments lie.

Dream fair virgins of delight,
And blest Elysian groves,
While the wand'ring shades of night,
Resemble your true loves.
Lulla lullaby, Lulla lullaby,
Your kisses, your blisses,
Send them by your wishes,
Although they be not nigh.

Thus dear damsels I do give,
Goodnight and so am gone,
With your hearts desires long live,
Still joy and never moan.
Lulla lullaby, Lulla lullaby,
Hast pleased you and eased you,
And sweet slumber seized you,
And now to bed I hie.

Fantasia

This fantasia and the one that follows are examples of more extended and sophisticated solo form and are fingered for lute tuning with the third string down to F♯ to avoid unnecessary technical difficulty.

This is from Mudarra's *Tres libros* (1546). It bears the full title "Fantasia, which imitates the harp of Ludovico," and is one of Mudarra's finest works, Mudarra commented rather accurately that this piece is "difficult until understood."

Suggested tempo is ♩ = 69.

1 *I have fingered this arpeggio style to give a more harp-like feeling. The original is in simple form on the first and second strings, with an open E throughout.*

2 *This is a difficult move, but it is necessary to sustain the chord and is possible with practice.*

3 *Sustain the B if possible. It can be done!*

4 *The section that follows is surprisingly modern and unexpected. Mudarra notes, "From here to near the end there are some discords, if played well they do not sound bad." The player is recommended not to slow down here, but to establish a tempo at the beginning slow enough to be consistent throughout.*

5 *This is a hard chord to manage in tempo, but the second finger helps when used as a guide.*

Alonso de Mudarra

108

Entrée De Luth

This French lute piece is from *Diverses pièces mises sur le luth* (Premier livre, Paris, 1611). Although not easy to play, it has great intensity of feeling and is well worth the effort. In spite of the title it sounds very much like a *tombeau* or lament.
Suggested tempo is ♩ = 63.

☐1 *Some practice is needed here, but it is worth it to hold the A.*

☐2 *It was necessary to simplify this measure to make it playable on the guitar. The original was*

☐3 *This is a stretch, but it is preferable to a complete change of position.*

☐4 *The half bar seven has to be changed from four strings to five, hence is shown twice.*

Robert Ballard

110

Fantasia

Although one of Dowland's more complex works, this fantasia will not be found to be as difficult as it looks owing to the lute tuning on the guitar. It is taken from Robert Dowland's *Variety of Lute Lessons* (1610).

In general, the music is clear in its intention, working from a majestic exposition through an exciting finale.

Suggested tempo is ♩ = 100.

1. *This is a hard trill for the third and fourth fingers, but the tablature shows all the notes on the same (second) string.*
2. *Lift the bar enough to allow the open E to sound while sustaining the G♯.*
3. *It is important to establish clearly the change of tempo. Possibly a slight hold here is appropriate, followed by a firm downbeat to begin the 6/8 time.*

3rd to F♯

John Dowland

111

My Love Hath Vowed

This song is from Rosseter's *Book of Ayres* (1601), which he shared with Campion. It has an interesting modal feeling in the first line and a most attractive balance of voice and instrument at the conclusion. It should go fairly fast.

1 *This fingering may seem strange at first, but with practise it seems to be the smoothest to negotiate the sixteenth notes in tempo.*

Thomas Campion

Had I foreseen what is ensued,
And what now with pain I prove,
Unhappy then I had eschewed,
This unkind event of love.
Maids foreknow their own undoing,
But fear not till all is done,
When a man alone is wooing.

Dissembling wretch to gain thy pleasure,
What didst thou not vow and swear?
So didst thou rob me of the treasure,
Which so long I held so dear.
Now thou prov'st to me a stranger,
Such is the vile guise of men,
When a woman is in danger.

Y loue hath vowd hee will forꝼake mee and I am al reaꝺie ꝼped.
Far oꞇ ther pro-miꝼe he did make me when he had my maiꞇ den head.

If ſuch danger be in playing, and ſport muſt to earneſt turne, I will go no more a maying.

115

Mr. Southcote's Pavan

This duet was originally for lyra-viol and appeared in Thomas Ford's *Musicke of Sundry Kindes* (1607). It is interestingly balanced between the parts and is well suited to two guitars. Unlike the other duets the individual parts are not musically coherent by themselves, and it is necessary to play both together for the musical idea to emerge. Suggested tempo is ♩= 69.

Thomas Ford

When From My Love

For the final song in this collection I have chosen one of my favorite pieces of Elizabethan frivolity. It should be performed at a good speed, which makes some demands on the player, particularly in the last line, but it is well worth the effort. This song is from Bartlet's *Book of Ayres,* published in 1606.

John Bartlet

When from my love I looked for love and kind af-fec-tions due,

Too well I found her vows to prove most faith-less and un-true.

For when I did ask her why, most sharp-ly she did re-ply, That

she with me did ne'er a-gree to love but jest-ing-ly.

Mark but the subtle policies that female lovers find,
Who love to fix their constancies like feathers in the wind.
Though they swear, vow, and protest,
That they love you chiefly best,
Yet by and by they'll all deny,
And say 'twas but in jest.